S0-FQM-948

INTO AFRICA

Adventures of a Missionary Kid

Monkey Hunting

Advantage™
INSPIRATIONAL

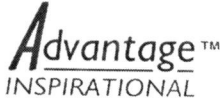

Beth Y. Lambert, M.D.

INTO AFRICA. Adventures of a Missionary Kid – Monkey Hunting by Beth Y. Lambert, M.D.
Copyright © 2008 by Beth Y. Lambert
All Rights Reserved.
ISBN: 1-59755-151-1

Published by: ADVANTAGE BOOKS™
www.advbookstore.com

This book and parts thereof may not be reproduced in any form, stored in a retrieval system or transmitted in any form by any means (electronic, mechanical, photocopy, recording or otherwise) without prior written permission of the author, except as provided by United States of America copyright law. Places in this story is real, however, some details have been fictionalized to fit the story

Scripture quotations marked NAS taken from the New American Standard Bible®, Copyright © 1960, 1962, 1963, 1968, 1971, 1972, 1973, 1975, 1977, 1995 by The Lockman Foundation Used by permission.

Library of Congress Control Number: 2008941792

Cover design by Pat Theriault
Illustrations by Tiffany Chupko

First Printing: December 2008
08 09 10 11 12 13 14   10 9 8 7 6 5 4 3 2 1
Printed in the United States of America

Into Africa

Dr. Jim Teeter, Beth, and Mae Teeter in Mattru, Sierra Leone in 1985

Dedicated to
Dr. James and Mae Teeter

Thank you for introducing me to missionary medicine and taking me to Sierra Leone as a medical student.

Your love of the Lord has encouraged me, your faithfulness and service have challenged me, and your legacy lives on as you inspire me to write.

Beth Y. Lambert, M.D.

Table of Contents

Chapter One 7
Into Africa

Chapter Two 13
Impressing Dad

Chapter Three 19
The Ferry

Chapter Four 23
The Mission Guest House

Chapter Five 27
Mission Rules

Chapter Six 33
Kevin

Chapter Seven 37
Dead Monkeys

Chapter Eight 43
Bumpe

Chapter Nine 47
Miss Maida Green

Chapter Ten 55
The Granddaddy Monkey

Chapter Eleven 61
Death and Life

Chapter Twelve.. 65
Angel

Chapter Thirteen 69
Bonded Together

Chapter One

Into Africa

Dave Rager's stomach churned and his hands trembled as he looked out the plane window. His excitement had been building as the plane descended into Africa, and now he could see the buildings of Freetown, the capital of Sierra Leone. He and his family were starting their first term as missionaries. Dave looked over at his mom, dad, and brother, and smiled when he saw them peering out the window, too.

"We'll be landing soon!" Dave exclaimed, and turned back to the plane window. He could see an endless jungle of small buildings, with a cluster of taller, larger concrete structures in the distance. Dave had studied about Sierra Leone with books from the library, as well as information from their mission agency. They would be going to Mattru Jong, a small town on the banks of the Jong River with low jungle surrounding it. His mom, Dr. Lori Rager, was a family practice doctor. She would work at the Mattru Mission Hospital along with another doctor and a number of American nurses. Dave's dad, Daniel, would be the new school principal at the Missionary Kid School in Mattru. Many of the students would be boarded there because their parents were missionaries far away or even in a neighboring country. Dave's six-year-old brother, Kevin, would be in first grade at the school, while twelve-year-old Dave was starting sixth grade.

Dave was excited to be a missionary kid. He loved adventure and the outdoors. Coming to Africa was a dream come true! He had many friends back home that he would miss, but he generally made friends easily, and figured he'd find someone at the missionary kid school he could pal around with. His parents had even asked him what he thought about the family becoming missionaries. They said that his opinion mattered just as much as their opinions. Dave remembered that he didn't hesitate to vote for the whole idea. He always loved hearing the missionaries at his church talk about leading others to Christ, and enduring many hardships along the way. Dave thought he and his family were up to that, and together they could take the mission field by storm! His parents had to calm down some of his expectations, but they were pleased with his excitement and acceptance of the change in their lives.

The plane's wheels soon touched down on the airstrip. Dave followed his family through the open hatch to a special stairway leading to the ground. He was suddenly hit by a blast of hot, muggy air. Big lights were coming on as the sun set. Dave paused and tried to take in the view, but someone behind him gave him a shove, propelling him down the stairs. He walked across some hot pavement, and then stepped into a crowded airport terminal behind his family.

Into Africa

Mr. Rager shouted above the confusion, "I think I see someone holding a sign with our name on it over there. Let's head that way. Stay close together, and don't let anyone grab your bags!"

Dave's heart pounded as he struggled against the throng of people headed in every direction. Fortunately, his dad was quite a bit taller than the Africans around him, his crew-cut brown hair covered by a ball cap, so it was easy to see him. It was difficult, however, to try to stay close to him. Dr. Rager, carrying Kevin, forced her way through the crowd to Dave's side.

"Here, stay ahead of me, and just keep going toward your dad. We don't want to get separated in this jungle of people!" she shouted above the noise as she maneuvered behind Dave.

Dave took a big breath, and almost choked on the smell of hundreds of peoples' body odor. He had been told that the Africans didn't wear deodorant, but he wasn't prepared for this! He was a little taller than average, but slender, so pushing his way through the people was a difficult task. The minutes seemed like hours as the people pressed in on him, and Dave began to panic. Suddenly, his dad stopped and motioned for his family. In a moment, they were together, breathing heavily in spite of the odor.

Mr. Rager smiled as he laid a hand on the shoulder of a black man standing next to him. "This is Albert, from the Mission Guest House. He'll help us through all this!"

Albert gave them a toothy, wide grin, and said, "Follow me!" as he headed off toward a large door. His few words sounded different to Dave, but in the din it was hard to figure out why. They followed Albert closely, watching him shout and wave his arms, clearing a path for them. They soon found themselves at Baggage Claim, and busied themselves finding their many pieces of luggage. There were ten large bags in all, which they loaded on a cart that Albert mysteriously obtained. The rest of their things had been shipped in crates by ship six weeks earlier. Albert guided them to Customs, and quickly found a uniformed man he seemed to know. The man nodded his head while Albert spoke and pointed at the Ragers. Dave felt like he was an animal in a zoo. The uniformed man stared at the four white people, his eyes coming to rest on Dr. Lori, whose short, blond hair seemed out of place in the sea of browns and blacks. The men smiled and shook hands, and then Albert motioned for the Ragers to come to an empty booth. By this time Dave felt sticky, with sweat dripping off his short brown hair. Kevin, too, was perspired, and looked like he had just played a basketball game. He resembled their father, with crew-cut hair also hidden by a ball cap. His slight, but lanky frame hung to Dr. Lori's side. She was average build, but she quickly and easily picked up Kevin into her arms. Dave often wondered how she could lift Kevin so smoothly. Well, she did like to work out and keep fit by running regularly, he thought. Maybe <u>he</u> could try lifting weights or something to make his

11

muscles grow. He looked down at his spindly arms and legs and sighed to himself.

A uniformed black lady appeared. "Passports, please."

Her English sounded different, too. Dave watched as she stamped each of their passports, and handed them all back at once. "Welcome to Sierra Leone!" she said with a smile showing the pure white teeth that seemed to be typical for these people.

Dave looked at his family, smiled, and joined them in saying, "Thanks!"

Dave thought, "I'm in Africa!"

Chapter Two

Impressing Dad

Dave, his family, and Albert wheeled the luggage cart to a Land Rover parked outside. People constantly pushed and shouted around them. Dave's parents had taken a course on the Mende language before leaving the US, and they had taught Dave a lot of what they had learned. He would learn more in school, but right now, he couldn't understand anything. The darkness seemed to intensify the feeling that hundreds of white eyes were looking at him. Dave shook his head to try to clear this ghostly image, and when he looked up again, he saw many African bodies attached to those eyes. He laughed out loud, but inside he felt frightened. He looked at his family. Kevin was clinging to his mom, who had her lips pulled tight, and his dad shuffled his feet like he did before an important game he was coaching. "We're all a little nervous," Dave thought. This was very different from America. Had they made a mistake in becoming missionaries? "God, please help me trust you and not be afraid," Dave silently prayed.

They loaded the Land Rover quickly, in spite of the many hands reaching for handouts. The Ragers had been told to ignore the begging, and definitely not to give the

Beth Y. Lambert, M.D.

people anything. Dave breathed a sigh of relief as they finally pulled away from the airport.

"The airport is on an island called Lunji, and we must go on the ferry to get across the Sierra Leone River to Freetown," Albert said.

Dave hung on as Albert took off, zipping around other vehicles. There sure didn't seem to be any driving laws! Dave stared in awe at a ramshackle truck, swaying back and forth with the weight of people, animals and luggage. There were even people hanging on the outside!

"Those are 'poda-podas', Dave," Albert said with his strange accent, seeming to read Dave's thoughts. "They're our buses or public transportation. The driver collects a fee for each item that comes on, so he doesn't care how many people or things are on his truck--the more on, the more money he gets!"

This time Dave thought to ask, "How come your English sounds different?"

Albert laughed. "I suppose I sound different to you because English is not my native tongue. I am a Temne, and that is the language I learned first. I also speak Creole, Mende, French, and a smattering of some other tribal languages. I learned to speak British English because Sierra Leone had been a British colony. We achieved our independence in April 1961..."

"Oh, I read about that," Dave interrupted. "You got into the UN right after that, and became a Republic in 1971."

"That's right, Dave!" Albert said with surprise. "You've done a bit of studying, eh?"

"Well, we tried to learn as much about our new home as we could," interjected Mr. Rager. "I enjoy studying other cultures and their history, and I guess Dave has inherited that knack, too."

Dave glowed at the compliment from his dad. This was the one thing they shared a liking for, and Dave tried hard to impress his dad with what he had learned. Sports were another matter, however, and Dave knew his dad was disappointed with his lack of athletic talent. Mr. Rager had been a basketball star in high school and college, and usually coached the school teams where he had taught or been the principal. Mr. Rager had worked many hours with Dave to try to teach him dribbling and shooting, but Dave tripped over his own feet running down the court, and couldn't even hit the backboard with the basketball. They finally called it quits after many a frustrating practice, and let Dave try his hand at some other sports. Baseball bored Dave. Soccer left him in the dust. Football crushed him. The list went on. Dave could sense his dad's disappointment as each sport was tried and given up. The only thing he had done fairly well was swimming, but there would be no pool in Mattru, no swim team, and no way to impress his dad. That was why Dave was surprised and proud of his dad's compliment about their shared enthusiasm for history. He'd make his dad more proud of him this way, he vowed! If only Kevin hadn't turned out to be so good at sports. Mr. Rager now spent a lot of time with Kevin, teaching him different sports and playing basketball with him. Dave missed the time that his dad used to spend with him and hoped to somehow prove himself to his dad. Maybe there would be something special that he could do in Mattru. Hmm...he'd learn the Mende language really well and maybe hold a Kids' Club to tell the African boys and girls about Jesus. His dad would be impressed with that. Or perhaps he could start a history club in school and his dad could be the faculty adviser. That would give them more time together again. Dave sighed and was yanked back to reality as the Land Rover jerked to a halt!

Beth Y. Lambert, M.D.

Chapter Three

The Ferry

"Ah, here is the line for the ferry," Albert said, while Dave breathed a sigh of relief.

People appeared out of nowhere and began displaying their products. Albert shook his head 'no' many times, then suddenly turned and asked, "Have you ever had sucking oranges?"

Mr. Rager said, "No."

Albert grinned and said, "Let me introduce you to one of our favorite treats!" He spoke to a lady at the side of the road, who nodded her head and pulled out five oranges. She cut a little off of one end on each of the oranges, and then handed them to Albert. He pulled out some coins and gave them to her. Others, seeing the exchange rushed over to Albert, but he waved them aside. "Here's how you eat a sucking orange," he said. He cupped the orange in his hand. By this time the Ragers could see that half of the rind's thickness had been peeled away. Albert placed the cut end at his mouth and sucked on it while he squeezed the orange. "Mmm....That tastes good!" he exclaimed.

Beth Y. Lambert, M.D.

The Ragers imitated their guide, and after a few misdirected squirts, got the hang of sucking on the special orange. The taste was sweet and refreshing, especially in the heat of the evening.

"Oh, they're loading the ferry now," Albert said and he drove slowly onto a large ferry, parking the Land Rover in line. "We can get out now. I'll stay with the car. There is an upper deck where you can sit down." He turned his head over his shoulder, indicating where they should go.

Dave jumped out of the Land Rover and ran to the stairs, leading his family. When he got up on the deck he looked up at the sky, and was amazed to see thousands of stars twinkling back at him. "Look at the stars everyone!" he exclaimed.

Even young Kevin breathed a sigh of "Ooh..." as the American family gazed upwards. "There are so many..." Kevin whispered.

Mr. Rager softly responded, "They don't have the many bright lights here like we have back home, so the stars are much more clear." He paused, and then said, "Our God is an awesome God!" He hummed a tune that went with the phrase, and Dave joined in. Soon the Ragers were singing out loud, attracting the stares of the other ferry riders.

A young black man approached them and smiled. "Our God is an awesome God..." he sang with a deep voice, blending in with the Ragers' voices. A few others came over and began to sing as well. Someone called another chorus name, and the singers switched to the new tune. After a few rounds of that song, a voice began another song. This went on for a half-hour while many looked on in bewilderment.

When they finally finished, the small group hugged and laughed. "Thanks for praising with us," Mr. Rager said. "It's always good to find other believers, even on a ferry!" They all laughed some more. "What are your names?" he asked.

Just then a whistle blew, and an African lady said, "We must get ready to leave the ferry. God bless you!" She and the others moved away before saying their names.

"I guess we'd better head back to Albert," Dr. Rager said. "That was sure incredible, though, wasn't it?" Her eyes gleamed and her face shone with joy. "It'd be great if it was always that easy to share the Lord with those around us!"

They made their way downstairs to Albert, and got in the Land Rover. "Hey, what was going on up on the deck?" Albert asked. "I thought I heard singing, you know, like choruses we sing in church. Was there a singing group up there?"

Dave answered him before anyone else could, "You missed the first performance of the Rager Four and Friends!" Dave grinned at Albert's puzzled look.

Albert thought for a moment, and then smiled. He shook his head and laughed. "You are going to do just fine here, folks, just fine!"

Chapter Four

The Mission Guest House

Albert wove in and out of traffic in Freetown. Soon they reached a tall house set up on a hill overlooking the city. Every inch of space seemed to be occupied, even on this steep hill. A guard let them through a metal gate. Albert pulled the Land Rover to the side and parked.

"Here we are!" he said with his wide grin. "Grab your overnight bags. We'll leave everything else in the car since you'll only be here two nights. The Guest House has a fence around it and a guard at the gate, so your other things will be safe."

Albert helped unload the few bags and then led them into a large foyer in the house.

"Welcome!" a cheery voice called, and a woman stepped out from a doorway, followed by a smiling man. "We're the Gilleses. I'm Norma and this is Jim. We run the Guest House. Put your bags down on the floor there and come on in to the sitting room. We have some snacks all ready for you, and your rooms ready, and we've been ready to meet you for some days now..." Norma rattled on while the Ragers made their way into a spacious room with trays of food set out on low tables. Albert called out a good-bye and was gone. The Ragers sat down and began to taste the treats and sip on some soda in bottles.

"Ah...that was just what we needed." Mr. Rager patted his stomach and leaned back in his chair after his family had finished eating. "Now, can you tell us what our travel schedule is? When will we get to Mattru?"

Jim Gilles stroked his balding head and replied, "Tomorrow we'll need to get your visas in order and do some paperwork for Dr. Lori to practice medicine here before you head up-country the next day. We purchased the items you requested to get you started housekeeping and will load them into your Land Rover--"

"Our Land Rover?" Dave interrupted excitedly.

Mr. Gilles smiled and asked, "Didn't you know that was going to be your car while you're here?"

"No, we didn't tell the children," Mr. Rager admitted.

"Wow! That's so neat!" Dave exclaimed.

"Anyhow, Albert will drive you to Bumpe the day after tomorrow. You'll stay there a few days to a week while the Harkins, our district supervisors, give you a bit of an orientation, then you'll head to Mattru maybe on the weekend," Mr. Gilles explained.

"You mean we won't get to Mattru 'til then!" Dave moaned. He was so excited about getting to his new home. Every day they were delayed would seem like an eternity.

His mom sighed and said, "We're all anxious to get to Mattru, Dave, but we need to follow the advice of the people who have been here a long time. This is quite a

Into Africa

new thing for us, and the more your dad and I understand, the better we'll do." Then she smiled and said, "Remember, we'll be here three years before returning to the States for furlough. A few days in Bumpe will hardly be remembered after three years, OK?"

Dave nodded, but he wasn't any happier.

Norma Gilles broke the glum atmosphere with her cheery voice, "Oh, you'll love visiting Bumpe. The Harkins have a pet monkey, and a large stream flows right at the edge of the compound that you can play and swim in. We always enjoy going to Bumpe and fellowshipping with the missionaries there. Wait 'til you meet Miss Maida!" She rolled her eyes and laughed, "That's an experience in itself!"

Dave sat straight up, thinking, "Who is Miss Maida?"

Into Africa

Chapter Five

Mission Rules

"Who's Miss Maida?" Dave asked quickly.

"She's the oldest missionary in Sierra Leone," Mr. Gilles replied, looking at his wife with scowling eyebrows as if he was upset that she brought up Miss Maida's name.

Dave gazed over at his parents to see if they had picked up on the subtle tension. His mom and dad both raised their eyebrows and stole glances at each other before Mr. Rager spoke up, "Is there a problem with Maida Green?"

So his parents knew this person! Why had they never mentioned her to Dave or his brother? The boys had learned the names of many of the other missionaries, but Dave didn't remember a Maida Green at all.

"Oh, she's harmless, Jim," Norma Gilles admonished. "I don't know why you concern yourself with her strange ways. The end result is that she's brought more people to the Lord than everyone else combined in Sierra Leone, and that should be what matters!" Mrs. Gilles finished with a hard resolve in her voice.

Beth Y. Lambert, M.D.

"Who's Miss Maida, and what's wrong with her?" Dave asked again, cautiously.

Mr. Gilles frowned and hesitantly replied, "Miss Maida Green is the oldest missionary in Sierra Leone, as I told you. It's just that her methods of bringing the lost to the Lord are a...um...a little different than what we, as a Mission, endorse."

Dave pressed him for more information, "What do you mean by 'different'?"

Mrs. Gilles took over, "Miss Maida dresses like the Africans, and eats like them, and talks Mende or Temne all the time. She goes to their pagan celebrations and visits them in their huts. She even has a gun and goes monkey hunting with them! The Mission Board has spoken to her about these things, but she continues to behave more like an African than a snobby missionary." Mrs. Gilles stuck up her nose in the air for emphasis. "I still say that what counts is that she makes friends with the Africans and leads them to the Lord. So what if she doesn't follow all the Mission Board rules and regulations!"

A strange silence followed and Dave felt uncomfortable. Then Kevin spoke up, "Mom, I'm tired. Can I go to bed?"

Mr. Gilles exclaimed, "Norma, where are our manners! These folks must be exhausted! Let's show them to their rooms. They'll have a busy day tomorrow!" With that, the Gilleses jumped up and ushered their guests up the stairs to nicely furnished bedrooms.

"Here's a big room for Dan and Dr. Lori," Mrs. Gilles said, without a hint of the conflict that had just transpired. "Do you want Kevin in with you?"

The Ragers nodded yes.

"Then, Dave, do you mind being up on the third floor by yourself?" Mrs. Gilles asked.

"Sure. I don't mind," Dave said as he followed Mr. Gilles up more steps and into a small room with a single bed. "What is the net for, Mr. Gilles?" he asked, pointing to a white net suspended over the bed on a frame.

"That's the mosquito netting. Pull it down and tuck it under the mattress like this," Mr. Gilles worked his way around the bed. "Leave just enough open for you to crawl in, and then tuck the net under from inside. We don't want you getting malaria from the mosquitoes. Over here is a balcony. Let me show you Freetown." He opened some French doors and stepped outside. Dave followed him and then gasped.

"Wow! You can really see from up here!" Dave gazed at the small lights shimmering below.

"I'll let you get to bed, Dave. Oh, there's a toilet and sink just across the hall, but if you want to shower, you'll have to go down to the second floor to the large bathroom there," Mr. Gilles said.

"Thanks, Mr. Gilles. Good night," Dave responded. Dave unpacked a few things and washed up before going outside on the balcony again. It was warm for being late at night. The lights seemed to be different--shimmering, perhaps, and not as bright, he thought. The noises were different, too. There weren't as many beeping horns and cars as in other cities back home in America. Here, he heard talking and music, yet he couldn't quite pick out anything he recognized. It came together as a loud hum.

Dave thought about the day's events. He smiled when he remembered his dad's compliment, then quickly his thoughts went to Miss Maida, and his face twisted as he wondered about this strange lady. Why did Mr. Gilles seem to dislike her, and why did Mrs. Gilles defend her? Even he and Kevin had been told that there were certain things the Mission Board frowned upon that were felt to detract from their Christian witness. As missionaries, the Ragers were asked to comply with these regulations. While they were in Sierra Leone, the Ragers were not to go to movies or dances. And beer and other alcohol were forbidden. None of them minded these rules. Mr. and Dr. Rager didn't drink anyhow or go dancing, and they rarely as a family went to movies. They were allowed to watch videos of 'quality' and appropriate subject matter, whatever that meant. But the Gilleses hadn't specifically mentioned Miss Maida doing any of those things. So what did Mr. Gilles mean when he said that Miss Maida did things differently than what the Board wanted? Why did the Board allow her to stay if she didn't obey the rules? Dave was no angel, but the idea of an adult blatantly disobeying the Mission Board seemed strange. Dave crawled into bed and tucked the mosquito netting in. He decided to stay as far away from Miss Maida as he could while they were at Bumpe. "Monkey hunting..." he mumbled sleepily. He wondered if one had to be athletic to hunt monkeys. Would this be another thing Dad and Kevin would do together, leaving him home alone? Kevin maybe was more athletic, but he was awfully shy, and cowered a bit with new things. Dave loved adventure, and felt he was more courageous than other boys his age. He'd convince his dad to take him monkey hunting somehow. Then Dave fell into a fitful sleep.

Chapter Six

Kevin

Dave awoke to a loud hum of noise. 'The monkeys are coming!' he thought as he jumped out of bed, only to find himself tangled in mosquito netting! He had been dreaming of monkey hunting. After untangling himself, he walked out onto the balcony to take in the sights. Small shacks and low concrete buildings stretched as far as he could see, and a yellow haze hung over the city.

"That's the 'harmatan'," a voice startled him out of his trance, and he turned to see Mrs. Gilles behind him. "Your parents have been up for a while and just left to get their paperwork done. Your mom asked me to get you up, but I see you already are!"

"What's a 'harmatan'?" Dave asked. "Is that smog?"

"No. A breeze from the Sahara Desert brings this dust, which settles over the city," Mrs. Gilles explained. "Are you ready for breakfast? Go ahead and get dressed. You and Kevin get a free day here at the Guest House. There are books and videos, and a basketball court in the yard...Lots to keep you busy..." Her voice faded off as she left Dave's room.

A basketball court. Great. Kevin will be sure to want to play there all day. And he was so good at it.

Maybe there's someone else here who'll play with him, but by the quiet Dave heard in the house, he doubted it. Why couldn't he be better at sports? Maybe he could hide in another room and read books. He'd try that.

Breakfast consisted of fresh fruits Dave had never seen before, along with homemade granola. Kevin seemed unusually quiet.

"You OK, Kev'?" Dave asked. He didn't mind his little brother most of the time. Dave just didn't like him hanging around all the time and showing off his athletic talent.

"Yeah," Kevin sighed. "I wish Mom and Dad would have taken us along with them."

Dave picked up on a tremor in Kevin's voice and went to his side. "It's OK. I'm here. Are you scared or something?" For all of Kevin's athletic ability, he was such a timid kid, and Dave knew that many situations frightened him. Dave enjoyed being the 'big' brother at those times, and tried to protect Kevin. Dave had a knack for saying the right things to encourage his little brother.

Kevin hung his head, hiding the tears Dave knew were there. Dave put his arm around Kevin's shoulders, and knelt down beside him.

"You know, Jesus helps us when we're afraid. Why don't we talk to him now?" Dave quietly asked.

Kevin nodded his head.

Into Africa

"Dear Jesus," Dave prayed, "we're here in Sierra Leone now, and a lot of this is very new to us, and sort of scary. Please help us to remember that You are with us and You'll protect us. In Jesus' name, Amen." Dave hugged his brother, and said, "Hey, I hear there's a basketball court in the yard. Do you want to go shoot some?"

Kevin lifted his wet eyes and smiled at his big brother, nodding his head.

As the two brothers made their way to the door outside, Mrs. Gilles peeked her head around the corner and winked at Dave when he went past. Dave smiled, then called to Kevin, "Maybe today I'll beat you at this game!"

Chapter Seven

Dead Monkeys

The next morning was busy as the Gilleses and Ragers loaded the Land Rover with groceries for the next month. Albert came and the group prayed for safety before heading away from the Mission Guest House. Albert steered the vehicle down the hill through the narrow streets. Now Dave could see open ditches along the roads, and an awful stench soon filled the car.

"What's that smell?" Dave asked.

Albert replied, "Those are open sewers. Most people do not have toilets."

Enough said. The Ragers looked at each other with raised eyebrows, and Dave gulped. Some adjustments to life here would be more difficult than others. Dave peered out the window at the crowded streets and the shacks that lined them. These people were really poor. Many did not wear shoes. Their clothes were torn and faded. Dave was not very fashion-conscious, but even he sighed at the strange clothing combinations. They wore plaids with stripes, flowers with polka dots, bright green with ugly orange. The shock of the poverty he saw made him feel sick. He thought about times he had complained about his clothes at home, and suddenly he felt a little ashamed. "God, I'm sorry I haven't always appreciated what You have given me," Dave prayed silently.

Finally, they got to the edge of town and sped up a little. The dirt road was full of potholes, and every bounce sent Dave into a piece of luggage.

"How long will it take us to reach Bumpe?" Dave asked, rubbing his ribs.

"Oh, usually 5 hours," Albert replied.

Dave groaned and Mr. Rager gave him a warning look. "Albert, can you tell us why those monkeys are along the road on those sticks?"

Dave sat up and looked out his window. Sure enough, there were small brown monkeys, obviously dead, hanging from sticks stuck in the ground at the edge of the road.

Albert said, "Those are monkeys for sale."

"But they're dead!" Dr. Lori exclaimed.

"Monkey meat is the only meat many of our people have to eat. Those who have guns and can hunt them make a living that way. This is usually how they sell them."

Dave saw his mom wince and her face turn white. He remembered his mom telling him once that monkeys carry many diseases, and that was one concern she had in coming to Sierra Leone. She knew there were many monkeys in various sections of the country. One reason Mattru had appealed to her was that there were not many monkeys in that particular area, and the people mainly ate fish from the river.

Into Africa

Albert continued, "Here and around Bumpe there are many Diana Monkeys. They live in groups called clans or troops with up to thirty in each. A clan is led by an old male." He paused and smiled, "We call him the 'granddaddy monkey'. He watches over his clan, going on ahead to make sure that everything is safe. Now, I've never seen this, but legend has it that the granddaddy monkey will attack if he thinks you will hurt any monkey in his clan."

Dave's eyes grew wide with excitement and interest. "Wow! Have you ever actually seen a granddaddy monkey, Albert?"

"Oh, a few times, I think I have from far away. Now a friend of mine lives near Bumpe where a number of monkey clans live. He says that he has seen a granddaddy monkey up real close. He's big, and he makes this grunting sound if he's mad." Albert tried to imitate it, "Hhur, ghur, ghur, hhur!"

"Mommy!" a small voice cried.

"It's OK, Kevin. Albert is just teasing us and just telling us stories to pass the time. I'm sure there is no such thing as a granddaddy monkey attacking anyone, isn't that right, Albert?" Dr. Rager spoke firmly with a cutting edge to her voice. She hated this talk of monkeys and now it had scared Kevin.

Albert stiffened as he understood the warning tone of her voice. He immediately smiled and pointed, saying, "Look, there's a lady with sucking oranges and other food. Anyone for a snack?"

Dave wanted to ask more about the monkeys, but he knew the subject was off limits now. Was he the only one to notice that Albert did not answer Dr. Rager? Had it all been just a story, or was it really true?

The Ragers and Albert enjoyed green bananas, beni-seed cakes, ground nuts (like peanuts), and sucking oranges. Albert pointed out ju-ju towns, where the villages are run by a witch doctor. Charms hung above the road as you entered the village, as well as when you leave. Albert talked a good part of the way, telling them many things about his country, but he never mentioned the monkeys again, even though they were displayed at the edge of the road the whole way. Mr. and Dr. Rager talked to Albert about how they hoped to share the love of God with these people, and tell them of Jesus and salvation. Kevin napped, and Dave dosed off with monkeys on his mind.

Beth Y. Lambert, M.D.

Chapter Eight

Bumpe

"We're here!"

Dave woke with a jerk. He had been dreaming of monkey hunting again. This time he had a gun and was hailed as a great man in his village because he shot the most monkeys. Was he an African in his dream? He didn't know. He shook his head to wake himself more. He looked out the window in amazement at the neat buildings shadowed by palm trees on the mission compound. He gingerly straightened his back, groaning at his sore ribs, but eager to get out of the Land Rover.

It was late afternoon, and a number of the missionaries were already strolling toward the vehicle. Albert grinned and shook the hand of a middle-aged man who arrived first. "Hello, Jon! It's good to see you again!"

"Albert! Greetings to you in the Lord! Was your journey uneventful?" the man responded.

"Oh, yes. Praise the Lord!" Albert turned toward the Ragers and said, "Here are the Ragers--Dan, Dr. Lori, Kevin, and Dave." He turned back to the man and introduced him. "This is Jon Harkins. He and his wife,

Laura, are in charge of the mission work in the whole country. Here is Laura now."

A thin lady with twinkling eyes approached and spoke, "Welcome to Bumpe! We're so glad to meet you and to have you join our mission team in Sierra Leone!"

"That's right!" exclaimed the booming voice of Jon Harkins. "We'll try to get you settled in and orient you to life here for a few days."

Other introductions were made. Dave looked anxiously for the strange character of Miss Maida Green, but she did not appear to be there. Whew! Dave relaxed and followed the Harkins into their home. Conversation about their trip and hassles getting all the right forms filled out in Freetown followed.

"Mrs. Gilles said you had a monkey," Dave interrupted, bored with the talk.

"Dave!" his mom cautioned.

"Ah, Mom! Their's is a pet. That's different, isn't it?" Dave asked, and looked at the Harkins.

"Rosy is out in the yard. We keep her in a cage most of the time so she doesn't mix with the native monkeys. She's had her shots and is very safe. You're welcome to get her out and play with her, if your parents say it's all right. You just have to put the leash on her," Laura Harkins said.

"Mom, p-lease," Dave stretched out the word hoping for approval. "You heard her. Rosy has had her shots."

Dr. Rager sighed, and reluctantly shook her head in affirmation. "Some things are going to be a little harder

Into Africa

for me to get used to. Go ahead, Dave. Take Kevin with you, and please be careful!"

Dave grinned and headed out the door with Kevin behind him. They found Rosy chattering in a cage in the yard. Dave found a leash hooked on the outside, gently opened the cage, and leashed Rosy by a bright blue collar around her neck. The monkey chittered and chattered excitedly while she climbed on Dave's shoulders. Kevin laughed and watched the funny antics of the monkey. They played with her for a while before their mom called to them to come in.

"It's time to eat, boys," Dr. Lori said. "We'll eat at a different home for lunches and suppers while we're here to help us get to know the other missionaries. Tonight, we're going to Miss Green's house."

Dave's face fell. "Mom, can't I just eat peanut butter and jelly here?"

His mom gave him a questioning look, "Of course not, Dave. You need to meet the others. Now, wash up so that we can head over to Miss Green's home."

Dave slumped, but followed Kevin to get washed. Well, maybe he could just stay real quiet and hope Miss Maida didn't notice him too much.

Chapter Nine

Miss Maida Green

Dave trailed behind his family and Mrs. Harkins as they approached a small building at the edge of the compound. Mrs. Harkins led the way and called out as she opened the front door, "Miss Maida, I've brought the Ragers!"

A slender black woman appeared, dressed in a colorful African wrap. "Miss Maida preparing meal," she said in broken English. "Please, come in. I am Susan." She bowed her head slightly. "Bua!"

Mrs. Harkins smiled and said, "Bua, Susan. I must get back home." She turned to the Ragers and said, "Make yourselves at home. Jon will come later to escort you back to our house."

The Ragers filed in through the door, and then Mrs. Harkins went out. Dave noticed right away that this was quite a different house. There were low tables and stools and few decorations. No rugs or carpets were on the floor. Some kerosene lamps hung on hooks on the wall, but candles lit most of the room.

"Bua! Bobbagahung?" said a slightly heavyset woman who came through a door. She also was dressed in a brightly colored wrap similar to Susan's. She smiled and reached out both hands to them. "Welcome to my home! I'm so glad to meet you! I've been working to make a special African meal for you, and missed greeting you when you first arrived. Please sit down! Dinner is ready to be served!"

Dave realized that they were to sit right where they had entered the house, on the low stools. He looked at his parents, who also seemed a bit surprised. Dave sat on the stool closest to the door while his family positioned themselves in the room. "This is weird and Miss Maida is weird," he thought. "I can't wait to get back to the Harkins."

Miss Maida's voice broke through Dave's thoughts, "You must be Dave. Would you mind helping me to bring the food in?"

Dave shrugged his shoulders and mumbled, "Sure." He got up and followed Miss Maida into the next room. The kitchen was a mess, with wooden bowls and spoons everywhere. He saw some cast iron pots sitting around, and the counter stained and marked. "Ugh!" he thought, and was glad his mom hadn't come in here.

Miss Maida picked up a huge bowl of white rice and gave it to Dave. "Here we go. Take this in for me." She spoke some other words, ending with, "Bissay, Dave. That means, 'thank you'."

Dave sighed and turned to go back into the other room. He set the bowl down on a table, then headed back to his chair when he heard, "Oh, Dave, I have a few more things to bring in." Miss Maida just wouldn't let him alone! She busied him with getting bottles of soft drinks for everyone.

Miss Maida finally seemed to be ready. "Pull your chairs in close. We're going to eat the Mende way--all together!"

Dave stared in horror as he realized they would all be eating from the same bowl! "Um," he said, "there doesn't seem to be enough room, I'll just wait 'til you all are done."

"Nonsense, Dave," Dr. Lori said, with a well-understood warning tone. "You'll sit here with the rest of us." She looked at him, and then winked and smiled. "This is new to us, Miss Maida. Could we use some individual bowls?"

"Oh, I'm sorry, I don't have any," Miss Maida replied with a smile. "I got so used to eating this way that I sort of lost my small bowls. At least I have forks for all of us!" Miss Maida looked around at her visitors, seemingly unaware of their uneasiness. "Let's thank the Lord for his bounty..." and she launched off into an African prayer. After sentences in another language, including some where Dave picked out 'Ragers', Miss Maida finally said, "Amen."

"Amen," Dave and his family responded.

Dave looked at his mom. She had raised her eyebrows at Mr. Rager. He just shrugged his shoulders, took his fork, and sampled the rice and topping.

Miss Maida and her helper dug into the food in the bowl in front of them. "I wanted to give you a good taste of African food. This is my favorite -- rice with dried fish and ground nut sauce," Miss Maida said.

Dave watched as his mom gingerly picked up the fork and took a small bite of the meal.

"Mmm, this is tasty," Dr. Lori replied, and motioned for Dave and Kevin to eat as well.

Dave reluctantly picked up his fork and took a small bite of rice. It was pretty bland. He got a little of the sauce on his next bite. "Ow, this is hot," he exclaimed, and reached for his soda bottle, taking a big swig. "What's in that?" he asked.

"Oh, you must have gotten one of the peppers. The Africans use a lot of peppers and spices to liven up their otherwise bland food. You'll get used to it as you eat more!" Miss Maida said.

"I doubt it," Dave thought, and ate small bites of the rice alone. Kevin, on the other hand, didn't seem to mind this new food and way of eating. He dug in with vigor as if he hadn't eaten in days! Mr. Rager seemed to be doing OK, but Dr. Lori was carefully eating around the fish and the sauce, Dave noticed.

Miss Maida talked endlessly as they ate. None of it interested Dave, so he daydreamed of jungles and monkeys only to be startled out of his thoughts by Miss Maida asking him, "Dave, would you like to go monkey hunting with me tonight?"

In his excitement at the prospect of actually going monkey hunting, Dave forgot his dislike for Miss Maida, and exclaimed, "Oh, wow! That would be great! Tonight? Really?"

Into Africa

"Wait a minute, Dave. I don't think that's a good idea," his mom interjected with firmness.

"Well, you can all come. I just thought Dave might be the most interested," Miss Maida explained. "I go every week or so to get monkeys for the African help here on the compound. Mr. Aruna usually goes with me. The weather is just right this evening."

"Please, Mom, I really want to go, please," Dave pleaded.

Dr. Lori spoke emphatically, "I don't like monkeys. You know that, Dave. I'd prefer that none of us go along. Thank you, Miss Maida." Her voice was cool toward the missionary.

Dave sighed. Oh, well. He knew better than to push his mom.

"Uh, Lori, could I speak to you a moment?" Mr. Rager asked. He motioned for her to follow him outside.

Dave looked at Miss Maida while straining to hear his parents' conversation. The missionary looked with downcast eyes at the rice bowl in front of her. Something finally had broken her optimism. Dave suddenly felt a little sad for her. She had been trying so hard to impress them with her knowledge and participation in the African culture. She didn't realize that her style was overbearing to the Rager family. Dave offered, "Maybe I can go another time, after we're settled in and Mom isn't so scared of monkeys?"

Miss Maida looked up at him and nodded. "Sure, Dave," she sighed, and slowly picked up the rice bowl from the table.

Into Africa

Dave's parents came in from outside at that moment. "Miss Maida," Mr. Rager said, "after discussing the monkey hunting invitation, we have decided to let Dave go with you."

Dave's eyes lit up with surprise. What had his dad said to his mom?

Mr. Rager continued, "As long as I can come along, and Dave stays far away from the shooting. This is something that has interested Dave, and will maybe help him to adjust to life in Africa." He turned and looked at Dr. Lori, and said, "We're having a lot of adjustments now, and our initial response is to shy away from the unknown or unfamiliar. Please excuse our tendency to stay with the familiar." He turned back to Miss Maida, who was smiling now. "Lori and Kevin will stay here, but Dave and I will be happy to accompany you." Dr. Lori smiled and nodded somewhat reluctantly in agreement.

"All right!" Dave exclaimed. "When can we leave?" All his misgivings about Miss Maida seemed to vanish.

"Right now!" Miss Maida responded, giving Dave a huge grin.

Beth Y. Lambert, M.D.

Chapter Ten

The Granddaddy Monkey

Dr. Lori and Kevin went back to the Harkins' house while Miss Maida and her helper cleaned the meal away. Dave was hopping from one foot to the other, impatiently waiting to go monkey hunting. Soon, Mr. Aruna, the school headmaster, arrived and they all got into Miss Maida's jeep.

"The coffee plantation is only a few kilometers from here," Miss Maida said.

"When did you start going monkey hunting, Miss Maida?" Dave asked.

"I learned to shoot a gun when I was a little girl on our farm. When I first came to Sierra Leone, it was a bit wilder in this region, and I felt better with my gun handy. Once I got to know my Mende friends here, I realized that many of them never got to eat meat. The Bible says that we need to feed those who are hungry, so I thought one way to get them to listen to the Gospel message was for me to somehow give them meat. One day one of the village elders, who was good at testing my Christianity, asked me to go monkey hunting with him. I did, and surprised him by shooting three monkeys." She laughed, "He didn't think women could hunt as good as men. He didn't get any monkeys that day!"

Mr. Rager and Dave laughed.

"So, I surprised him further by offering him the monkeys I had shot. No one ever gave away monkey meat in the village. It gave me an opportunity to witness to him, and a few weeks later, he was the first convert to Christianity. Since then, many have come to know the Lord, and," she chuckled, "many have just gotten some free monkey meat. Either way, I believe Jesus would want me to continue, so I keep monkey hunting. Some take advantage of it, but the Lord is in charge of what happens. I just have to obey him."

Dave marveled at the faith of the old missionary lady. Maybe she was right, after all! Dave wondered if these things were what the Mission Board and Mr. Gilles didn't agree with. Dave pondered what Miss Maida had said. He remembered the story of the sheep and the goats that Jesus had told his disciples in Matthew 25:35-40: *'For I was hungry, and you gave Me something to eat...' Then the righteous will answer Him, saying, 'Lord, when did we see You hungry...?' And the King will answer and say to them, 'Truly I say to you, to the extent that you did it to one of these brothers of Mine, even the least of them, you did it to Me.'* Dave smiled to himself. He knew what he thought of Miss Maida now.

"Do you eat the monkey meat, too, Miss Maida?" Mr. Rager asked.

Miss Maida hesitated before responding quietly, "No, I don't eat monkey meat. It has to do with a bad dream the devil pushes at me--" She stopped abruptly, and then changed the subject. "Here we are at the plantation, folks!"

Dave felt a little uneasy. He wondered what Miss Maida's dream was about, but they quickly got going on a trail, and Dave soon forgot about it.

Miss Maida led the way into the low jungle of the coffee plantation, and whispered, "The monkeys come in at night to sleep in the trees in the coffee plantation. If we time it right, we get up the path before they come, and shoot them as they head into the coffee trees. Once we shoot, the others will swing the other direction pretty fast, so we have to keep cool and aim well or we'll lose sight of them. One false shot can ruin the entire hunting trip." She stopped in the path and looked at Dave, "This is the best place for you to stay." She turned to Mr. Rager and said, "Would you mind coming up the path just a little bit, and at my signal move into the brush to herd the monkeys towards us? We'll go up the path to a place we usually see the monkeys. Dave should be plenty safe here." And with that, Miss Maida and Mr. Aruna vanished into the darkness, with Mr. Rager trailing behind them.

Dave sighed as he watched the others leave. The jungle was very quiet, but Dave imagined hearing low grunts in the bushes to the side of him. He laughed to himself and pictured Miss Maida shooting a big granddaddy monkey. He should have asked her if what

Albert had told them was true. She would know if there were granddaddy monkeys, and if they attacked. He shivered a little at the scary thought, but shrugged his shoulders and sighed.

"Ghurmph."

There it was again. It was a grunting of sorts. Dave had never heard anything like it. It was in the bushes on the far side of him. He started to call to his dad when he heard Miss Maida call softly, then the jungle seemed to come alive with chattering and monkey calls.

"Bang!" And a few seconds later, "Bang, bang!" Miss Maida and Mr. Aruna were shooting at the monkeys. The monkeys started to shriek and swing through the trees all around Dave!

"Ghurmph, g---hurmph!"

Dave jumped as the grunting got closer to him. Monkeys were swinging in the trees above him and the air was filled with shrieks and calls. What should he do?

Dave turned around, trembling and his heart pounding. "Dad! Dad! Help! Where are you? Jesus, help me!"

"G-hurmph, gghhur, ghurmph!"

Dave turned in time to see a large shape break through the brush and lunge toward him at amazing speed!

"Ah!" Dave screamed. He tried to move but couldn't, and watched helplessly as a huge monkey jumped at him!

Into Africa

Beth Y. Lambert, M.D.

Chapter Eleven

Death and Life

Dave felt the weight of the large beast fall on him at the same time as he heard, "Crack!" A gun went off nearby.

The monkey's breath was hot, and Dave felt the slobber from its mouth on his cheek. "I'm going to die, he thought" as he screamed and fell to the ground with the beast on top of him.

"Dave! Dave!" he heard someone call.

"Are those the angels coming to take me to Jesus," Dave wondered? He felt no pain, no struggle. He even felt the weight of the granddaddy monkey fall off of him. Dave felt a peace come over him. He wasn't afraid of dying. He had always been taught that God would give him peace when he needed it, and he knew that God was doing just that. What would heaven be like? Would he see Jesus soon? He became aware of some voices again. One voice was calling him. "Jesus, I'm here," Dave tried to say, but no words came out.

"Dave! Are you OK? Son, speak to me! Oh, God! Please don't let him die!" Dave heard a familiar voice crying. It seemed so far away. He felt his body being lifted gently and held. A voice was sobbing, "Please, don't let him die, Lord! Oh, please help us!"

Dave slowly opened his eyes. His dad was holding him in his arms, with tears streaming down his face. "Dad," Dave murmured.

"Dave!" Mr. Rager cried. "You're alive! Oh, thank you, Lord! Can you move? Are you hurt?"

"I don't know." Dave held up his arms and then bent them. He did the same with his legs, and sat up in his dad's lap. "I think I'm OK, but I thought I was dead. What happened?" Dave then noticed a large monkey motionless on the ground in front of him.

"Agh! The monkey... it attacked me...I remember...What happened to it?" Dave's words came out in a stream of thoughts. He shook in his dad's arms.

"My gun shot it," a trembling voice said.

Dave looked up to see Miss Maida step into the faint light on the path. The moon was shining brightly now, washing away the ghastly shadows of the night.

Miss Maida stepped over to the beast and nudged it with her shoe. She then closed her eyes and lifted her head toward heaven. Her lips moved silently as her one hand clutched her chest. She breathed deeply and opened her eyes. "Praise God for His protection! Dave, are you hurt?"

"I think I'm OK, but I feel weird. It's like my stomach is sick all over my body," Dave struggled to explain.

Into Africa

"Well, you had quite a shock. Let's get you back to the Mission Compound so your mom can check you out," Miss Maida directed.

Mr. Rager lifted Dave up off the ground, and then hoisted him easily into his arms. "Just try to relax, Dave. Take some deep breaths and close your eyes. We'll be to the jeep in just a few minutes. You've been very brave, son. I'm proud of you!"

Dave hugged his dad, and realized that his dad loved him regardless of what sport he could or couldn't play. He felt a sense of peace in his dad's arms, knowing that he never had to do anything to impress his dad anymore! "It's like the Father's love," he thought. "It doesn't matter what I do-- God still loves me." That made him think of Miss Maida, and he felt ashamed for judging her even before he met her. He should love her because she loves the Lord. Dave caught Miss Maida's eye and smiled. Miss Maida smiled back at him.

Miss Maida and Mr. Rager headed back down the trail. Mr. Aruna silently knelt by the dead monkey. He pulled out a knife and slit the tail midway back, then pushed the split tail around the monkey's head. He picked up the monkey by the tail, having made an instant carrying handle. He hurried down the trail and caught up with the others as they were putting Dave in the jeep. He quietly opened the back hatch, laid his gun down, and lifted the large, dead monkey into the back.

Chapter Twelve

Angel

The ride back to the Mission Compound went quickly, and Dave was feeling better by the time they arrived. The Africans, eager to see how the hunt had gone, soon surrounded the jeep. Miss Maida held up her hand to silence the group, which by now also included the Harkins and Dr. Lori.

"We had a very unusual hunt tonight, and by God's great protection, avoided tragedy," Miss Maida said quietly. The crowd murmured as Mr. Aruna pulled the granddaddy monkey from the back of the jeep.

"We've all heard rumors of the old granddaddy monkeys", Miss Maida continued, "and how, when their clan is threatened, they will attack. I have hunted monkeys many years with no problem, so I never considered those stories to be true. But, tonight, this granddaddy attacked and would have killed Dave if it hadn't been for God's provision!"

The Africans moaned and cried, many lifting their hands up to the heavens. Dr. Lori couldn't believe what she was hearing and cried out, "Dave! Where's Dave? Is he hurt?" and she ran to the jeep.

Dave slowly got out of the back seat with Mr. Rager, and the crowd cheered. Dr. Lori hugged him, and, with tears running down her face, looked at her husband, and then Dave with a million questions in her eyes. She sighed and held Dave out at arm's length, and said, "Dave, are you OK?"

"I'm all right, Mom. I guess I'm a little shaken up, but I'm OK," Dave responded.

"Miss Maida, what happened?" someone called out.

Miss Maida took a big breath and exhaled. "Mr. Aruna and I went to shoot the monkeys, just like we always do. But when I went to pull the trigger, it wouldn't go. I felt like I was being pushed back down the trail. Somehow I got back to where Dave was. I don't remember passing Mr. Rager. It was almost as if someone else was controlling my body. Then something…" she paused, "… or *someone* held my arms and raised the gun. The gun went off. I heard Dave screaming and Mr. Rager ran right past me like I wasn't there. That's when I saw the granddaddy monkey lying on top of Dave, dead." Miss Maida looked around at those gathered there, and proclaimed, "I believe God's angels were with us tonight, and because of our God's power, Dave is unharmed!"

The crowd murmured to each other, and someone started clapping.

Dave hugged his parents, amazed at the story he had just heard. Wow, angels had saved him!

Into Africa

At that moment an old African voice quieted the people in their native tongue. Dave turned to see a very old man sitting on a stump. The man pointed to Dave, then raised his arms to the sky and spoke excitedly in Mende. Everyone listened intently, and many nodded their heads in agreement with his words.

Miss Maida came to Dave's side and explained, "Patrick was the village witch doctor long ago, but finally came to know the Lord after years of persistent prayer. He just said, 'Your body was saved from death tonight, but it is more important that Jesus saves your soul from eternal death.' "

The old man took the granddaddy monkey from Mr. Aruna, lifted it up in the air, and cried out in Mende again. Miss Maida laughed and translated, "He said, 'Jesus has saved us from Satan, the granddaddy monkey of them all!'"

The people cheered, and then huddled around Miss Maida, Dave and his parents. They touched the gun the angel used, and poked Dave all over to see that he truly was OK. This time the crowd didn't bother Dave. He smiled and thought again, "Wow! I was saved by an angel!"

Chapter Thirteen

Bonded Together

The group finally dispersed back to their homes, leaving the Ragers and Miss Maida alone. There was an uncomfortable silence before Miss Maida spoke, "I'm sorry I put Dave in such danger. Nothing has ever happened like that, and it frightened me. God used the situation and showed us a miracle, but maybe that was His mercy and grace taking over when I shouldn't have...well...I was just trying to...uh..." Miss Maida paused, trying to find the right words.

Dr. Lori interrupted and said softly, "You were only trying to welcome us to our new home in the best way you knew how---by involving us in the culture you are so much a part of now. There's nothing wrong with that. We all knew there would be dangers here that we weren't used to, but there are dangers everywhere! What matters is that we trust God in whatever situation we are in. Dave could just as easily been bitten by a rattlesnake on one of our hikes back home. It is God who protects us, and sometimes He uses His angels to do just that!" Dr. Lori smiled at Miss Maida, who nodded and bowed her head briefly.

Dave sensed something special had just occurred between his mom and Miss Maida. He knew his mom had just taken a big step in trusting God to protect them in this new environment. She was used to being in control and helping her patients and family. Now she was acknowledging God's providence in a new way. Dave glanced back over at Miss Maida. She was wiping her eyes. Mr. Rager had moved in between Dr. Lori and Miss Maida, and put his arms around each of them, pulling them together in a hug. Dave smiled, and said, "Hey, what about me!" The other three laughed as Dave completed the circle and embraced the two women.

As the new friends grinned at each other, Miss Maida sighed deeply and said, "I want to tell you something I have never told anyone before. Dave, you had asked me why I didn't eat monkey meat, and I didn't want to tell you. Now I can." She folded her hands, sat on a stump, and continued, "When I first came to Bumpe, and no one knew the Lord, I started having a nightmare. I figured Satan wasn't too happy about me being here. I've had that nightmare time and time again. I had heard about granddaddy monkeys, but, like I told you, I thought it was all just stories the Africans were telling me. I didn't think the stories were true. But, I would dream that a granddaddy monkey attacked me. He bit and clawed me until I woke up in a sweat. For some reason, I was still able to hunt the monkeys, but I could never bring myself to eat the meat---like that would really offend the granddaddy, and he would be after me." She shook her head and sighed, "I know it doesn't make a lot of sense, but that was my reaction. Tonight, my nightmare came to life, and that ol' granddaddy was defeated! Some say that once you live out a nightmare, it will never bother you again. That'll suit me just fine!" Miss Maida laughed and the Ragers joined in.

Miss Maida stood up and said, "You folks certainly must be tired. Uh, where is Kevin?" She looked around curiously.

Dr. Lori spoke up, "He could hardly keep his eyes open, waiting for you to return, and he fell asleep on the couch at the Harkins'. We carried him into bed just before you came back. He will be so disappointed to have missed all this excitement! Oh, Dave, you were to stay at Miss Maida's house. We took your bag over there. Are you OK with that, or do you want to come and sleep with us? This has been an unusual night, and we certainly wouldn't mind if you'd want to squeeze in with your dad and me."

Dave straightened up and looked over at Miss Maida. Just a few hours ago he didn't want to have anything to do with her, and now, well, God had used her to save his life. She seemed to be a pretty neat lady, after all.

"Nah, I'm OK with Miss Maida," he said with a smile. "With angels by her side, I think her house is pretty safe!"

Miss Maida's shoulders rose as she smiled and sighed, "Thanks, Dave! You and I have a bond in the

Beth Y. Lambert, M.D.

Lord that is pretty unique. I think we're going to be good friends!"

"Well, then, good night," Dr. Lori called as she and Mr. Rager turned to go. "See you in the morning!"

Miss Maida reached out for Dave, and he took her hand as they walked into her house.

"It's late, and I think you must be tired, Dave," Miss Maida said tenderly as she showed him the room he was to sleep in. "Shall we have prayer, and then you can get to bed?"

Dave nodded and tried to stifle a yawn.

Miss Maida took his hand, closed her eyes, and prayed, "Father, you have shown us Your great power and mercy this evening. Thank you for Your protection. Thank you for bringing the Ragers safely to Sierra Leone. May you bless the ministry they will have in Mattru. Now, watch over us as we sleep. In Jesus' name, Amen."

"Good night, Miss Maida!" Dave crawled into bed and Miss Maida helped him tuck in the mosquito netting. As she left, she turned out the kerosene lamp and closed the door.

Dave sighed happily. What a day! In spite of his near-death experience, he felt wonderful. And he hadn't even gotten to Mattru yet! What other adventures were up ahead? He was excited about living in Sierra Leone, and grateful for the new friends he and his family had made. As he fell asleep, he thanked God for Miss Maida, his rescue by angels, and what he had learned. Dave drifted off to sleep thinking, "Next time, I'll shoot that monkey!"

'For though I am free from all men, I have made myself a slave to all that I might win the more. And to the Jews I became as a Jew, that I might win Jews; to those who are under the Law, as under the Law, though not being myself under the Law, that I might win those who are under the Law; to those who are without law, as without law, though not being without the law of God but under the law of Christ, that I might win those who are without law. To the weak I became weak, that I might win the weak; I have become all things to all men, that I may by all means save some. And I do all things for the sake of the gospel, that I may become a fellow-partaker of it.'

1 Corinthians 9: 19 23 [NAS]

Dr. Beth Lambert is available for speaking engagements and personal appearances. For more information contact:

Dr. Beth Lambert
C/O Advantage Books
P.O. Box 160847
Altamonte Springs, Florida   32716

To purchase additional copies of this book or other books published by Advantage Books call our toll free order number at:
1-888-383-3110 (Book Orders Only)

or visit our bookstore website at:
www.advbookstore.com

*A*dvantage
BOOKS

Longwood, Florida, USA
"we bring dreams to life"™
www.advbooks.com